C.9

J
970
H

Hook, Jason.
  Sitting Bull and the Plains Indians /
... 1987.   (Card 2)

1. Sitting Bull, Chief of the Sioux,
1831-1890. 2. Indians of North
America--Great Plains. I. Hook,
Richard, ill. II. Title III. Series

22 MAR 89   15581536   NOBExc 86-70992r882

SITTING BULL
AND THE
PLAINS INDIANS

Jason Hook

Illustrated by Richard Hook

The Bookwright Press
New York●1987

LIFE AND TIMES

Further titles are in preparation

First published in the
United States in 1987 by
The Bookwright Press
387 Park Avenue South
New York, NY 10016

First published in 1986 by
Wayland (Publishers) Ltd
61 Western Road, Hove
East Sussex BN3 1JD, England

© Copyright 1986 Wayland (Publishers) Ltd

ISBN: 0-531-18012-2
Library of Congress Catalog Card Number: 86-70992

Phototypeset by Planagraphic Typesetters
Printed by Sagdos S.p.A., Italy

Contents

The publishers are aware of the tendency to refer to those peoples who occupied North America before the arrival of Columbus as native Americans. In the context of the present book it is felt this would be inappropriate, and its subjects are referred to either by the names of their tribes, their tribal groupings, or generically as Indians.

1 THE STORY OF SITTING BULL

A warrior's name

The Sioux war party waited eagerly in ambush, as enemy warriors from the Crow tribe approached. Among the Sioux was a boy known as Slow, on his first raid. He had been born among the Hunkpapa Sioux, near Grand River, in 1831 — only fourteen years before. Slow had daubed red paint over his horse, yellow paint over his body, and clutched in his hand a slender willow wand, called a "coupstick."

Unable to restrain himself, Slow dashed from hiding, galloping recklessly toward the startled Crow warriors. One of them leapt from his horse and aimed an arrow at the boy; but before he could release it, Slow struck him

with his coupstick. By touching the enemy, he counted what was called a "coup." Although the older warriors killed a number of the Crows, Slow, through counting "first coup," had won the greatest honor.

Back at the Sioux camp, Slow's father was filled with pride. Some years earlier, he and three companions had been sitting around a fire roasting freshly killed meat. Suddenly, they had seen a lumbering buffalo bull approaching. It was muttering four names: Sitting Bull, Jumping Bull, Bull Standing With Cow and Lone Bull. Because he was able to understand the buffalo's strange speech, Slow's father took the sacred names for his own use.

Now that Slow had proved his courage, his father gave him the name that he had originally taken himself. He declared to the camp that his son would now be known as *Tatanka Iyotake* — "Sitting Bull."

Below *A lone buffalo bull approached Slow's father and spoke the name "Sitting Bull."*

Above *In 1872, Sitting Bull fought against troops escorting surveyors along the Yellowstone River. To prove his courage and power, he sat between the opposing lines of soldiers and Indians and calmly smoked his pipe.*

Sioux chief

Sitting Bull's reputation as a warrior grew rapidly. At the age of 25, he was shot in the foot, which left him with a permanent limp. He killed his assailant, however, a Crow chief, and was made leader of an elite group of warriors called the "Midnight Strong Hearts." A year later, he mercifully spared the life of a helpless Assiniboin boy — later named Jumping Bull — whom he then adopted in a ritual called the *Hunka* ceremony.

Sitting Bull was also known as a mystic, and a vision he had of an eagle, which he interpreted to mean that he would become a leader of his people, came true in 1867. At this time the Sioux faced a growing threat from the white man. Tribal leaders gathered in a vast lodge and

Sitting Bull, 36 years old, was presented with a magnificent war bonnet of eagle feathers. Recognized as the protector of their traditional way of life, Sitting Bull became the chief around whom the Sioux rallied.

His beliefs were demonstrated during the visit of a Jesuit priest, Father De Smet, in 1868. Asked to consider exchanging the Sioux's ancestral hunting grounds for rations, Sitting Bull replied, "I will not have my people robbed . . . we can feed ourselves."

His fierce independence was threatened, however, by the appearance of parties of white surveyors in the 1870s who threatened the Sioux lands. When his courage was questioned by another Indian during a fight with one of the parties, Sitting Bull conceived a marvelous gesture. Laying down his weapons, he strolled out and sat between the lines of soldiers and Indians. Ignoring the flying bullets, he filled his pipe, contentedly smoked it, and scraped out the bowl, before ambling back to safety.

Above *This tobacco pipe was made for both everyday and ceremonial use.*

A vision of victory

In the early summer of 1876 a spectacular camp of Sioux, Cheyenne, Assiniboin and Arapaho Indians joined up with Sitting Bull's Hunkpapa band. Their numbers swelled to more than 10,000, as they gathered, hunting buffalo. They had united to defend the Black Hills, the sacred center of their lands, where the whites had discovered gold in 1874.

On June 14, as soldiers marched toward his camp, Sitting Bull performed a spectacular ceremony at the Hunkpapa Sun Dance. As he prayed, a hundred pieces of flesh were cut from his arms. Then, his body stained red with a "scarlet blanket" of blood, he danced, without food or water, gazing at the sun until noon the next day. Exhausted, he fainted and received a vision of defeated white soldiers.

His vision was fulfilled on June 25, 1876, when Indian warriors, fortified by Sitting Bull's "medicine," wiped out General George Armstrong Custer's command at the battle of the Little Bighorn.

Soon after this great victory, the Indian camp broke up and Sitting Bull, after skirmishing with Colonel "Bear Coat" Miles, led a large following into "Grandmother" Queen Victoria's Canada, arriving early in 1877. He found temporary refuge behind the stone-heaped border, but his disillusioned followers, growing cold and hungry, slowly drifted home. When the Canadians refused to allocate him a reservation, Sitting Bull cried out despairingly, "I am thrown away." He led less than 200 followers south. Finally, on July 19, he surrendered at Fort Buford, handing over his rifle via his eight-year-old son, Crawford.

Above *A contemporary photograph of Sitting Bull.*

Left *At the Sioux Sun Dance ceremony in 1876, Sitting Bull sang to the Great Spirit, as his adopted brother Jumping Bull cut 50 pieces of flesh from each of his arms.*

"No Indians left but me!"

American promises of a pardon were forgotten and Sitting Bull, now 50, was held prisoner at Fort Randall. On May 10, 1883, he was released to the Standing Rock Agency. There, he clashed with agent James "White Hair" McLaughlin, who was working to destroy the Indian traditions Sitting Bull loved. McLaughlin refused to recognize the old chief's leadership.

Sitting Bull, however, maintained much of his influence, partly through his fame with the American public. He undertook a lecture tour in 1884, and in 1885 traveled with the Wild West Show of Buffalo Bill Cody, who afterward presented him with a circus horse.

In 1888, Sitting Bull victoriously united Indian chiefs in rejecting government attempts to buy Sioux lands. But it was a short-lived victory. Next year, McLaughlin

Above *Sitting Bull with Buffalo Bill Cody, a photograph taken in 1885.*

persuaded chiefs like John Grass and Gall to sell. Asked what the Indians thought of this, Sitting Bull exclaimed, "Indians! There are no Indians left but me!"

On December 12, 1890, McLaughlin was ordered to arrest Sitting Bull, who was unfairly blamed for stirring up the Indians by leading the new Ghost Dance religion. Before dawn on December 15, Lieutenant Bullhead led forty-three Indian police — called "Metal Breasts" because of their badges — to the 59-year-old chief's cabin. Outside, tribal rivalries flared into violence. Six Metal Breasts, Sitting Bull, and seven of his followers including Jumping Bull, were killed. As the great chief fell dying, his circus horse danced through its tricks.

Sitting Bull — warrior, visionary and chief — fought proudly for his people's right to live freely in their own lands. His death spared him the humiliation of the white man's ration lines, while symbolizing the end of the traditional Indian existence he had struggled to uphold.

Below *At dawn on December 15, 1890, Sitting Bull was shot dead by members of the Indian police. He had foreseen his own death when, some days before, he had heard a meadowlark sing "the Sioux will kill you."*

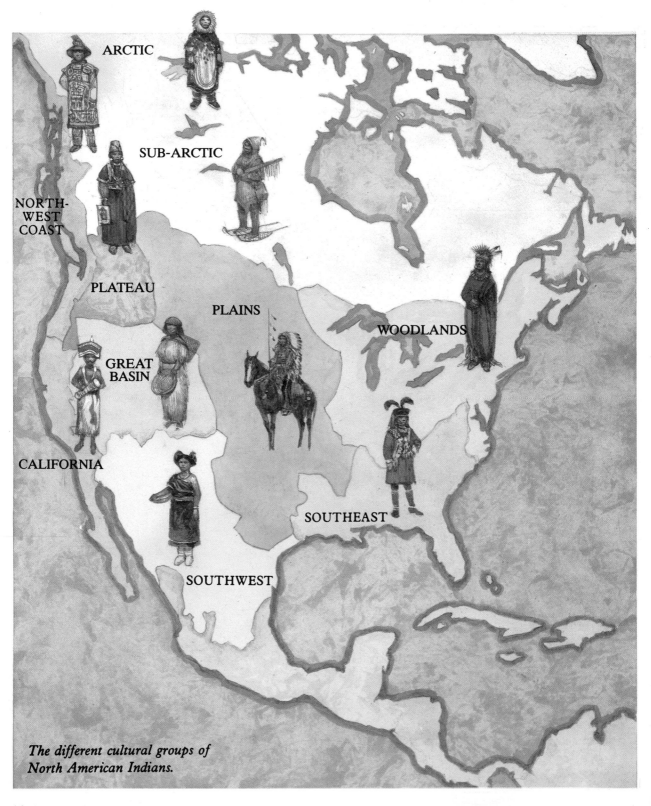

ARCTIC

SUB-ARCTIC

NORTH-
WEST
COAST

PLATEAU

PLAINS

WOODLANDS

GREAT
BASIN

CALIFORNIA

SOUTHEAST

SOUTHWEST

The different cultural groups of North American Indians.

2 THE NORTH AMERICAN INDIANS

Origins

It is thought that the first inhabitants of North America arrived here over 20,000 years ago. They crossed from Asia when the seas shrank, exposing a "land-bridge" between the two continents at the Bering Strait. As these wandering hunters roamed across America's changing landscape, they divided gradually into the different North American Indian groups. They had lived here for thousands of years before Columbus "discovered" America less than 500 years ago.

In the southwest lived farmers — called Pueblos after their great stone towns — and roaming hunters of the mountains and deserts, called Apaches. Farther north, plateau tribes like the Nez Percé hunted, fished and foraged for wild plants, sometimes stalking buffalo on the plains. In California, the Indians lived in simple bark or reed houses and were superb basket weavers. The Indians of the temperate northwest coast lived in large wooden houses, ate mainly fish, and carved magnificent totem-poles. In the far north, sub-Arctic tribes fished and hunted moose and caribou, while the frozen lands of the Arctic itself belonged to the Inuits.

In the east lay the "woodlands," teeming with wild game and fish, and home for powerful warrior nations like the Iroquois. Tribes here lived in villages when planting or harvesting crops. They used treebark to build their spacious longhouses or smaller wigwams, and to construct canoes.

Within these areas, each individual tribe had its own fascinating characteristics. Another distinct group of tribes lived in the heart of North America, on the Great Plains — home of the buffalo.

Above *The map shows the migration of the North American Indians' earliest ancestors, thought to have occurred more than 20,000 years ago. They crossed from Asia to North America when the seas were frozen, by way of the Bering Strait.*

Below *A riverside village of the Haida people, of what is now British Columbia on the west coast of Canada.*

The buffalo hunters

The plains of North America were once a vast, flat, or windswept grassland, broken occasionally by wooded river valleys, and roamed by huge herds of buffalo. Before Columbus, only a few nomadic Indian tribes lived there. Their only "domesticated" animal was the dog so, as they could carry few possessions, the Indians' wandering life was hard.

The white man's arrival in the 1600s brought a number of new tribes to the plains. Many were forced to flee westward from the woodlands by those tribes that first acquired guns from the whites. The plentiful buffalo also tempted these Indians to venture onto the plains, as did the arrival of horses with the Spanish.

Several of these tribes lived at the eastern edge of the grasslands on the prairies, until they fully adapted to plains life. There, they practiced the agriculture of the woodlands, while also hunting buffalo. Some tribes, like

the Mandan, retained this prairie culture, living in villages of dome-shaped homes called earth lodges.

Nine tribes made up the true Plains Indians. They were buffalo hunters, living a nomadic life in lodges called tepees, or *tipis*. They divided their warriors into societies and conducted a ceremony called the Sun Dance. A particularly powerful tribe was called the Lakota or Teton Sioux. They were related to the Yankton and Santee Sioux tribes in the east. The Teton Sioux were divided into seven sub-tribes: the Brulé, Miniconjou, Oglala, Oohenonpah, Sans Arc, Sihasapa and Hunkpapa. From them came famous warriors like Red Cloud, Crazy Horse and, of course, Sitting Bull.

Below *Some of the people from different tribes on the plains: 1 an Assiniboin warrior from pre-horse days; 2 a woman from the Crow tribe, with her child safely tucked into a cradleboard; 3 a Sioux woman; 4 a Comanche warrior; 5 a Cheyenne warrior; 6 a man from the Blackfoot tribe in typical "upright" bonnet.*

3 "THE HAIRY MAN FROM THE EAST"

The first white men

In 1620, the Pilgrim Fathers landed at Plymouth, Massachusetts, to join the growing European settlements of northeast America. The astonishing arrival of an English-speaking Indian called Samoset saved them from starvation. He introduced the settlers to Massasoit, chief of the Wampanoag tribe, and to an Indian named Squanto who helped them fish and grow corn.

As the colonies prospered, however, thousands more settlers arrived. Their farms soon spread through the woodlands. Whites stole land already cleared by the Indians, and drove the tribes, whom they regarded as "heathen savages," ever westward.

In 1622, settlers were massacred by Indians in Virginia, where Jamestown, Britain's first permanent colony, had been founded in 1607. Merciless retaliation followed, and the Pequot tribe was completely destroyed. In 1675, Metacom, the son of Massasoit, angry at English contempt for the Indians who had originally befriended them, led an alliance of tribes to war. Hundreds died when Metacom was defeated. His wife and son, like many Indians, were sold into slavery.

Twice more the Indians united to defend their lands. In 1763, an Ottawa chief, Pontiac, sent round the war belt of *wampum,* but was defeated when his union of tribes broke up. In 1812, another great tribal union, organized by the brilliant Shawnee leader Tecumseh, supported the British against the now independent Americans. Tecumseh's death in 1813 ended the dream of a separate Indian nation. "The hairy man from the East," as Sioux chief Standing Bear later called the white man, was now free to venture west across the plains.

Above *Woodland Indians approach the members of an early European settlement in the northeast.*

Traders and trappers

Above *Hernando de Soto, who led the Spanish expedition of 1539.*

Spanish exploration in the south, led by Hernando de Soto in 1539, and Francisco de Coronado in 1540, saw the first white contact with Indians on the plains. The Spanish settlement of New Mexico was marked by terrible cruelty, as they forced slavery and the Christian God upon the Pueblo Indians. With the Spaniards, though, came horses, released in great numbers when the Pueblos revolted in 1680. As horses spread from the southwest, guns were acquired by tribes in the northeast.

The northeast was also the scene of the fur trade. The English Hudson Bay Company, formed in 1670 to rival French traders, pushed frontiers westward to Blackfoot Indian lands. Trading posts were established where the Indians exchanged pelts for the tobacco, metal tools, blankets, beads, guns and ammunition that dramatically altered their lives. In 1800, a beaver pelt might be exchanged for 70 grams (1½ lbs) of gunpowder, twelve pelts for a gun. However, traders also brought whisky and disease. Smallpox, for example, decimated the Indians, who had no natural resistance to such illnesses.

In 1804, Meriwether Lewis and William Clark led an incredible 13,000-kilometer (8,000 mile) expedition across the Rockies to the Pacific. They were followed by rough white trappers, "mountain men" like Jim Bridger and Kit Carson, trapping for beaver pelts to trade at an annual "rendezvous." Their era had ended by 1840, but many of them became scouts and guides, leading settlers along their old trails, as the great westward migration began.

Right *The Indians brought valuable hides to the trading posts to trade for the settlers' goods.*

Above *The Oregon Trail crossed half the continent of North America.*

4 CLAIMING MOTHER EARTH

The Oregon Trail

As the Eastern settlements spread inland, trails branched across the plains to white settlements in the west. Three major routes began at Independence, Missouri. The first was a trade route, the Santa Fé Trail, started in 1822, which cut through Kiowa and Comanche territory on its way to present-day New Mexico.

The great emigrant route, though, was the 3,200 kilometer (2,000 mile) Oregon Trail, along which the first wagon train lumbered in 1841. After 1843, families of emigrants, their wagons laden with provisions, furniture and livestock, and hauled by mules or oxen, crossed in thousands. Since their wheels dug deep ruts into the soil, new tracks had to be started alongside, and the Oregon Trail became etched on the landscape.

It passed through the hunting grounds of the Crow, Cheyenne and Sioux, particularly those who had traveled south to trade. The whites chopped down groves of trees and exhausted the rich grasses that provided grazing. They slaughtered the sacred buffalo, taking only choice cuts and wasting much of the meat, and they left terrible diseases in their wake. Outraged by such destruction of their lands, some Indians demanded gifts from the wagon trains. Others attacked the white settlers and some of the unfortunate emigrants lost their lives. To protect them, the American army transformed Laramie trading post into a fort in 1849.

During the 1849 gold rush, the third route, the California Trail, was flooded with tens of thousands of miners. As the newcomers brutally decimated the California Indians, the plains tribes prepared to defend their lands.

Below *A Plains Indian warrior watches as a wagon train travels through his tribe's hunting grounds on its route along the Oregon Trail.*

Treaties

In 1851, a great gathering of tribes met to sign the Fort Laramie treaty. It was one of many treaties drawn up, and often broken, by the whites. William Penn's 1686 Walking Purchase, for example, bought as much land from the Delaware Indians as a man could walk in one and a half days. It was transformed in 1736 when Penn's heirs hired a runner to pace out a 96.5 kilometer (60 mile) stretch. In 1830, President Jackson broke numerous promises by enforcing the Indian Removal Act. Southeastern tribes were marched from their lands to "Indian Territory" in the west. One in four Cherokees died on the journey they called the "Trail of Tears."

The Laramie treaty showed how little the whites

understood Indian beliefs. They asked the tribes to respect each other's boundaries; but the Plains Indians loved to roam and fight, and the idea of drawing lines across the sacred "Mother Earth" meant nothing to them. The whites also asked the Indians to elect chiefs who would be responsible for whole tribes; but Indian leaders were advisers not dictators, and an Oglala, for example, could not speak for a Hunkpapa even though they were both from the Sioux. Treaties were often broken by tribes who had not signed them, and friendly Indians were killed for the actions of "hostiles."

Many Indians "touched the pen" simply to receive a share of promised gifts. They had no idea that this permitted whites to build roads and forts on their lands, or that the white man's government would reduce a promised fifty years of gifts to only ten.

Below *Indian chiefs and United States officials negotiate a treaty.*

5 LIFE ON THE PLAINS

Sacred dog — the horse

Knowledge of horses, acquired originally from the Spanish by the Pueblos around 1600, spread across the plains from tribe to tribe. As the Indians learned to ride, they acquired horses by trading, capturing wild "mustangs" and raiding both the whites and each other for them. In this way the horse spread northward across the continent.

The Plains Indians christened this wondrous creature "sacred dog," for to them it had all the uses of a huge, mild-tempered dog. They adopted it so eagerly that soon plains life was centered on the horse. Children rode from

infancy, men collected great herds as a measure of
influence; horses were even offered as gifts with
marriage proposals.

The horse brought great prosperity to the plains tribes.
The threat of starvation was reduced, since they could
travel farther after game, hunt more successfully and
carry greater food supplies. The *travois*, a carrying frame
that had originally been dragged by dogs, was enlarged
so that hides, larger lodge covers, even children, could be
hauled along behind the horse.

The horse also brought about an age of constant
warfare. Tribes extended their hunting grounds into
enemy territory, and warriors demonstrated their bravery
by raiding for horses from their enemies' camps. In short,
the horse transformed the Plains Indians. When the
whites threatened the plains in the 1850s, they were
confronted not by a ragged, pedestrian people, but by
proud nations, which boasted some of the finest
horseback warriors that ever lived.

Above *Mounted warriors watch
for enemies as a Plains Indian
band moves camp. Lodges and
belongings are carried on* travois,
hauled behind their horses.

Chasing the buffalo

The millions of buffalo that wandered their homeland supplied the Plains Indians with their every need. Tepees and clothing came from the buffalo's hide, tools from its bones, glue from its hooves. Every part was used, and buffalo meat fed the tribes.

Hunting buffalo was a difficult task before the arrival of horses. Hunters used wolfskin disguises to approach herds, and wore snowshoes when driving buffalo into winter snowdrifts. To kill larger numbers, families hid along a V-shaped run, and scared buffalo toward a stockade or cliff. A whole tribe working together, could surround the buffalo in a great circle, before closing in for the kill.

On horseback, the Indians developed a form of hunting called the chase, in which hunters lined up in hiding, mounted on their finest horses, called buffalo-runners. At a signal, they galloped after the herd. In the fury of thundering hooves, the Indians' horsemanship was tested to the full. Each rider, usually armed with a bow, used knee-pressure to guide his mount close to his prey. He then shot an arrow at the buffalo's right haunch. Further shots were often required to fell the buffalo, but skillful hunters could account for several animals in one chase.

The Plains Indians hunted other game, like elk, and gathered wild plants that often gave their names to particular months. July, for example, was known by the Sioux as the "moon of cherries blackening." Survival, though, depended on the buffalo.

Below *Indian hunters ride among a stampeding herd during the furious excitement of a buffalo chase.*

The hunting band

The plains tribes spent most of the year divided into "hunting bands" — small camps often containing only twenty or thirty tepees. Within the Hunkpapa tribe, for example, the bands were called the Devil's Medicine Man, Half Breech-clout, Fresh Meat Necklace, Sore Backs, Those That Carry Bad Bows, and Sleepy Kettle.

These bands roamed constantly after buffalo. In the fall, they hunted for meat to feed them through the winter. As the bad weather set in, they followed the buffalo into sheltered river valleys, where each band set up its winter camp. When spring arrived, the buffalo wandered back onto the open plains, gathering into large herds. There they were followed by the various hunting

bands, who camped together as their paths crossed. Only in summer, when huge buffalo herds could provide plentiful meat in one area, did the bands pitch their tepees in one great tribal camp.

The tepee was a tilted cone of wooden poles, wrapped with a heavy cover of buffalo hides. It could withstand rain and strong winds, and was heated by a central fire, the smoke from which tanned the tepee's peak as it drifted out of two smoke flaps or "ears." A tepee-liner prevented drafts, while ventilation was provided by rolling up the lodge cover. Tepees were pitched facing east to honor the rising sun, and comfort inside them was ensured by strict rules.

The tepee could be easily transported by horses and quickly erected or dismantled by two Indian women. This mobility was vital to a nomadic, warlike people.

Above *Painted tepees cluster together in a Blackfoot camp.*

33

Camp life

A Plains Indian camp was a lively scene. While the men relaxed and children played, the women went about their work. Some returned to camp laden with firewood, water, wild roots or berries. Others cooked buffalo meat after a successful hunt.

Smoke drifted amid the tepees as meat roasted on skewers hung over fires, or stewed in a buffalo-stomach pot containing vegetables and hot rocks to make the water boil. Around the camp stood wooden frames on which the women hung strips of meat to dry into *jerky*. Women also sat pounding such meat together with berries and fat, to make *pemmican*, which, stored in rawhide wallets called *parfleches*, could last the Indians through the winter.

Animal hides would be staked to the ground with women working over them. Some used fleshing tools to clean skins, or prepared rawhide by scraping them to an even thickness. Others rubbed in a tanning mixture of animal brains, and pulled hides back and forth across a rope, softening the skins so that they could be used for clothing.

Having prepared the hides, the women crafted them into new tepee covers, clothing and containers. They demonstrated their skills by adorning their work with beautiful decorations, using porcupine quills — until the white men brought them colorful beads. Clearly, while the men enjoyed the dangers of hunting and war, it was the women who were at the center of camp life.

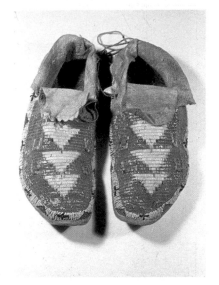

Above *These moccasins, made of buffalo hide, are decorated with both beads and porcupine quills.*

Left *An Indian girl brings firewood to warm the tepee, while a baby watches from a cradleboard strapped to its mother's back. The woman in the foreground is scraping flesh from a stretched buffalo hide and, in the background, meat is being hung out to dry.*

Above *An Indian offers up a prayer to the Sacred Powers, which surround him in the natural beauty of his world.*

6   A SACRED WORLD

Wakan Tanka — the Great Spirit

"Oh Great Spirit, be merciful to me that my people may live!" So an Indian boy prayed to the Sacred Powers during his "vision quest," the ritual through which he sought a vision from his Gods.

At a lonely spot, naked save for a breech-clout, and a buffalo robe for warmth at night, the vision seeker cried continuously in prayer to the Great Spirit — called, by the Sioux, *Wakan Tanka*. He consumed no food or water during his ordeal, which often lasted for four days — this being considered the sacred number. Visions came in many forms, for the Great Spirit was believed to be part of everything. Birds and animals often bestowed the spiritual power called "medicine" that the visionary sought during his quest.

The Indian's life was guided by his medicine. To preserve it, he made under the guidance of his elders a "medicine bundle," such as a sacred shield or pipe, and learned special ceremonies and songs. A boy who received medicine from the eagle might represent his power by wrapping talons in an eagle-skin bundle, and wearing an eagle feather in his hair to protect him in battle.

Because their religion was so constant and natural, the Indians offered up frequent prayers, often carried by the smoke of a sacred pipe, and treated their world reverently. Sitting Bull used to walk barefoot across the morning's dewy grass to "hear the very heart of the Holy Earth."

Below *Illustrated here is a collection of Crow medicine items. From left to right: a warrior's eagle-talon medicine bundle; a medicine pipe believed to bring good luck; and a medicine shield of buffalo hide, decorated with gruesome painted designs, feathers and a bird's head.*

The Sun Dance

Above *This warrior is about to enter a sweat lodge, before joining one of his tribe's important ceremonies.*

The plains camp was often enlivened by religious, social and warrior dances, and rituals surrounding such things as tribal medicine bundles, tobacco growing, initiation into societies and the reaching of adulthood.

The greatest ceremony among most tribes was the Sun Dance, held when the tribe united in the summer. Its rituals were conducted in a great lodge, centered around a forked cottonwood tree. This tree first had to be scouted for, as though it were an enemy, before it was ritually felled and carried to the lodge to be raised.

Many rituals of the Sun Dance, such as the consumption of huge quantities of buffalo tongues, took place in the lodge, but the most spectacular were the performances of the "torture dancers." They, like all important participants, prepared by fasting and purifying themselves in a "sweat lodge." This was a small dome, usually made of willow saplings covered with hides, in which scalding steam was created by pouring water onto red-hot rocks.

Adorned with paint and wearing sage wreaths, the dancers blew on eagle-bone whistles as they bobbed on their toes, staring continuously at the cottonwood tree or the sun. Some pierced their chests with skewers, attached by ropes to the tree, and fell back on them or were lifted clean off the ground, until the skewers tore free. This sacrifice, like the whole Sun Dance, appealed for the Great Spirit's blessing upon the tribe, and renewed tribal morale before the hunting bands divided for another year.

Right *In the medicine lodge, a Blackfoot man wearing a breech-clout, sacred white paint, and sage grass around his ankles, wrists and head, tortures himself as he performs the Sun Dance ceremony. He blows on an eagle-bone whistle while trying to pull the skewers — attached by ropes to the central pole — free from his chest.*

Raiding for scalps and horses

Below *Two "Model 1866" Winchester rifles, decorated with brass studs. Indian riders found the shorter version especially suitable for firing from horseback.*

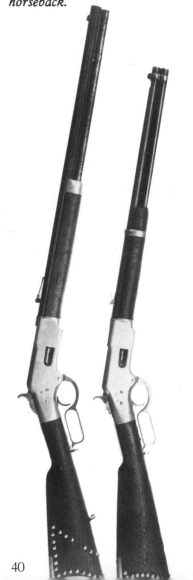

The Plains Indians warred continuously, to gain and defend hunting grounds, and avenge the deaths of relatives. Horse raids were frequent, usually involving a small party who rode deep into an enemy tribe's lands. Under cover of darkness they drove off a camp's horses, silently cutting free the finest mounts from outside their owners' tepees. Slowed by the stolen herd, the fleeing raiders often had to turn and fight their pursuers. Successful raids, though, won numerous horses and asserted a tribe's strength over its enemies.

Warriors also raided for scalps, often for vengeance, and the larger, better-organized raids were a constant threat to every hunting band.

The plains fighters, seeking always to win themselves great prestige, proved their courage with reckless displays of daring. Counting coup by striking an opponent a harmless blow, and other war honors such as snatching an enemy's gun, often received greater credit than killing a man. Such fighting methods clashed with the tactics of the white soldiers, whose cause was further helped by the hostility between feuding tribes.

The war medicine — charms, painted shields, body and face paint — that protected a warrior, contributed to his magnificent appearance. Crazy Horse, for example, saw his regalia in a vision. Hanging a small stone behind one ear, a hawk skin in his hair, he painted a red lightning streak down his face and spots representing hail on his body, before sprinkling himself and his horse with dust.

Right *Two warriors in full war costume, on painted ponies, fight a mounted battle. The Crow warrior, in magnificent grizzly bear headdress, is "counting coup" upon his Sioux enemy by touching him with his "coupstick."*

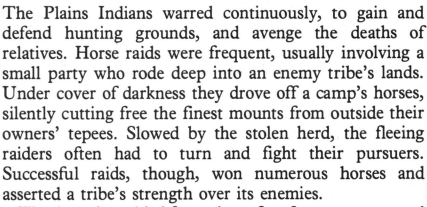

Strong Hearts

Warriors painted records of their battles on buffalo robes and tepees, and decorated their costumes with symbols of war honors. A shirt adorned with a painted hand and fringes of hair or ermine, for instance, might show the owner had triumphed in hand-to-hand combat, and was a renowned warrior. Feathers, displayed in the hair or on flags and shields, often represented coups, and a tribe's greatest warriors proclaimed themselves by wearing magnificent war bonnets of eagle feathers.

Wide-eyed youngsters, watching such finely dressed warriors proudly recount their coups, longed for the day when they too could continue the warrior tradition of their people.

Other regalia was worn to show membership in a warrior society. Societies provided meeting places for a tribe's fighting men, contact between peace chiefs and war chiefs, and forces to police the summer camp — preventing individual hunters from scaring the buffalo away. While some tribes had "ungraded," fiercely competitive warrior societies, others graded them so that a warrior could gradually progress from the least to the most prestigious.

Sitting Bull, as a sash-wearer in the Strong Hearts society, wore a buffalo-horn bonnet, and a scarlet sash which he staked down in battle. Held in place by it, he would fight until he defeated an enemy or was released by a comrade. Such insignia increased a man's prestige, until he gained enough influence to become a chief of his society, band or tribe.

Above *This picture, drawn by an Oglala Sioux, shows a dance in honor of the horse, and is connected with membership in a horse-owners' society.*

Left *Sitting Bull declares his intention to stand ground against the oncoming Crow warriors by staking down the end of his Strong Hearts sash.*

8 THE WAR PATH
Red Cloud's War

The 1851 Laramie treaty did not preserve peace for long. In 1854, Lieutenant John L. Grattan and thirty soldiers were killed after attacking a Sioux camp and attempting to arrest a Miniconjou Indian, High Forehead, for killing an emigrant's stray cow. The army soon retaliated.

To the east, Indian grievances flared in 1862 when hundreds of settlers were killed by Santee Sioux warriors in the Minnesota Massacre. Thirty-eight suspected Indian ringleaders were later hanged.

Following expeditions in 1865, Colonel Henry B. Carrington brought troops in 1866 to build forts along the Bozeman Trail, a branch of the Oregon Trail that cut through Indian hunting grounds on the Powder River.

Below *Captain Fetterman's troops fall under a hail of arrows as Indian warriors charge from hiding.*

Ignoring Oglala leader Red Cloud's protests, Carrington commenced building Fort Phil Kearney. The Sioux, led by Red Cloud, raided constantly, and on December 12, 1866, a party of woodcutters from the completed fort were attacked. A relief force of eighty men was sent out, led by Captain Fetterman, who had once boasted, "Give me eighty men and I'll ride through the whole Sioux nation." The soldiers were lured over a high ridge by ten decoys including Crazy Horse. Beyond view of the fort, all of Fetterman's men were killed as more than 1,000 Sioux, Cheyenne and Arapaho warriors emerged from hiding.

Despite Indian losses at the Wagon Box and Hayfield fights of August 1867, their resistance eventually won Red Cloud's War. In 1868, the Bozeman Trail forts were abandoned and burned, and Red Cloud touched the pen that signed another treaty.

Above *Red Cloud, leader of the Oglala Sioux in the struggle to hold the Powder River country for his own people.*

Black Kettle of the Cheyennes

While their northern brothers fought alongside Red Cloud, the Southern Cheyenne were threatened by settlers and gold miners. Soldiers attacked the Cheyennes, accusing them of stealing cattle, and warriors responded by raiding settlements. Many were restrained, though, by Chief Black Kettle, who told Governor Evans of Colorado, "All we ask is that we may have peace with the whites. We want to hold you by the hand. You are our Father."

In the winter of 1864, Black Kettle camped at Sand Creek, under guaranteed protection from Fort Lyon. At dawn on November 29, however, Colonel J. M. Chivington attacked with over 700 soldiers, including some murderous "100-day volunteers" — white settlers who enjoyed killing Indians. Black Kettle raised a huge

American flag above his tepee to indicate friendship; but soldiers shot over 130 Cheyenne, mostly women and children, including one little girl as she was sent from hiding waving a white flag. The dead were scalped and mutilated.

Black Kettle survived the terrible massacre, and remained peaceful. He signed away lands under the 1865 "Peace Policy," and the 1867 Medicine Lodge Creek treaty. In 1868, he sheltered Cheyennes who had been raiding, and camped, again under soldiers' protection, by Washita River.

One morning in November, Black Kettle's followers awoke to the cry of "Soldiers!," as Lieutenant-Colonel "Long Hair" Custer's troops, pursuing "hostiles," attacked the camp. Black Kettle and his wife were shot from their pony and fell dead into the river. The old chief had paid fully for trusting white men who wished to subdue the Indians, not by friendship, but by force.

CRAZY HORSE'S ATTACK (4PM)

CHEYENNES

GALL'S ATTACK

BRULES

SANS ARCS

CUSTER'S ROUTE

OGLALLAS

BLACKFOOT
SIOUX

MINICONJOUS

LITTLE BIGHORN RIVER

HUNKPAPAS

GALL ATTACKS RENO (3PM)

RENO'S ADVANCE AND RETREAT

BENTEEN'S POSITION

The Little Bighorn

After signing the 1868 Laramie treaty, Red Cloud retired to a reservation. Many Sioux and Cheyenne bands, though, remained independent of the whites, roaming lands guaranteed to them by the treaty.

In 1874, "Long Hair" Custer's expedition into this territory discovered gold in the Black Hills — an area proudly held by the Indians as the spiritual heart of their lands. By 1875, nearly 1,000 miners were illegally camped there, and the Indian warriors had painted for war. The government, unable to persuade angry reservation chiefs to sell the Black Hills, ordered the independent bands to report to the agencies by January 31, 1876, or be considered "hostile." The Indians, though, could not travel in the harsh winter weather, without terrible hardship. Many did not turn up. So, in March, the Indians united behind Sitting Bull to defend their lands.

On June 17, 1876, over 1,000 Indian warriors attacked General Crook's soldiers and Crow and Shoshoni scouts at a place called the Rosebud. The Indians' spirits were high, and Crook was forced to withdraw. On June 25, Custer's soldiers attacked the Indian camp at the Little Bighorn. Major Reno's initial charge from the south was fought off while the Indian women and children fled. Custer then attacked from the east, but Indians led by a Hunkpapa warrior called Gall forced him northward. As Custer made for higher ground, warriors surged up before him, Crazy Horse at their head. Sitting Bull's medicine was strong, and dust filled the air as the Indians engulfed Custer's troops "like bees swarming out of a hive." Custer's entire command of 215 men was wiped out.

Above *General George Armstrong Custer, who commanded the white soldiers' attack at the battle of the Little Bighorn.*

Left *The map shows how the Indians defeated Custer's forces at the battle of the Little Bighorn.*
Red arrows = Indians; Blue arrows = Custer's command; Green arrows = Reno's command; Purple arrows = Benteen's command.

49

9 A DEFEATED PEOPLE

The warriors surrender

After Custer's defeat, soldiers came in even greater numbers. The Indians had no idea how many white men there were, and as they continued to cross the plains, bringing guns, alcohol, and disease, Indian defeat became inevitable.

It was caused largely by the slaughter of the buffalo, for hides, their choice tongues, and meat to feed railroad workers. Professional hunters with high-powered rifles littered the plains with rotting buffalo carcasses. By 1872, over a million animals were being killed each year. Military leaders knew that the Plains Indians would starve without the buffalo, and as they became reliant on the white man's rations, so the Indians were forced to submit to the white man's will.

In September 1876, the government at last took control of the Black Hills. They forced agreement from reservation Indians by telling them to "sign or starve." In May 1877, Crazy Horse surrendered, and in September he was stabbed to death by a soldier, while his arms were held by an Indian policeman. That same year, Chief Joseph led his mistreated Nez Percés on a 2,750 kilometer (1,700 mile) flight from the army, toward Sitting Bull in Canada. He surrendered only 50 kilometers (30 miles) from the border, declaring sadly, "From where the sun now stands, I will fight no more forever."

The last "hostiles," Geronimo and his tiny band of Apaches, surrendered in 1886. The white man had won North America, and Red Cloud later reflected: "They made us many promises, more than I can remember, but they never kept but one; they promised to take our land, and they took it."

Above *The illustration shows some of the great Indian leaders who played an important part in the wars on the plains. From left to right: Gall and Sitting Bull of the Hunkpapa Sioux; Red Cloud of the Oglala Sioux; Joseph of the Nez Percé; Geronimo of the Apaches; and Quanah Parker, a noted Comanche leader.*

The reservations

The defeated tribes were each given an area of land called a reservation, run by agents from the Indian Bureau. In 1887, the Dawes Act divided these tribal lands into 65 hectare (160 acre) plots for each family, to force them to farm like white people. Settlers bought the remaining lands, and by 1889 the Sioux had lost over 4 million hectares (10 million acres). One Sioux, Yellow Hair, gave a ball of earth to the Pine Ridge agent, saying, "We have given up nearly all our land, and you had better take the balance now; and here I hand it to you."

Below *The monotony of life around the agency posts led to misery and despair.*

Reservation life was miserable. The Indians' religion lost its meaning, and was attacked by white teachers and Christian missionaries, while ceremonies like the Sun Dance were banned. The Indians became homesick for their old, and often faraway, lands, and felt trapped by reservation boundaries. "I love to roam over the prairies," said the Kiowa, Satanta. "There I feel free and happy, but when we settle down, we grow pale and die."

The warriors regarded farming as women's work, and anyway, the land they were given was often unsuitable for crops. So, they traded a life of chasing buffalo through the changing seasons for one of despair, standing in agency lines, with ration tickets, to receive poor quality food and clothing.

Many government agents were corrupt, and sold Indian rations for their own profit. Even those few agents who were honest often found the job of forcing a strange lifestyle upon the Indians impossible.

10   THE DISPOSSESSED

The Ghost Dance

The Ghost Dance began on January 1, 1889, when Wovoka, a Paiute Indian, received a vision during an eclipse of the sun. Wovoka told the Indians not to fight, but instead to dance the shuffling Ghost Dance, clasping hands in a circle, and chanting until they fell into a trance. Then they would see their dead relatives, who would soon bring back the buffalo. The world would be renewed, the whites destroyed and the Indians would live in harmony.

The religion spread rapidly, carried by apostles like Kicking Bear, a Miniconjou Indian, who brought it to Sitting Bull. The despairing Sioux clutched at the Ghost Dance's promises and began wearing brightly decorated

"ghost shirts," to protect them against the soldiers' bullets. This, and the great emotion of the Ghost Dance, alarmed the whites.

In November 1890, Pine Ridge agent Daniel F. Royer, who the Sioux called "Young Man Afraid of Indians," frantically called in the army. Over 3,000 Indians fled to the Badlands in North Dakota, and, led by Kicking Bear and Short Bull, danced in the snow. On December 15, amid the panic, Sitting Bull was killed.

His followers joined Big Foot's Miniconjou band. Heading toward the Badlands, the 350 Indians met the 7th Cavalry, and surrendered. They were held prisoners at Wounded Knee Creek. On December 29, as troops disarmed the Indians, a medicine man began a Ghost Dance, and a shot was fired. The army's rapid-firing Hotchkiss cannons opened up, killing about 180 men, women and children.

On New Year's Day, 1891, soldiers buried the frozen bodies. The promise of the Ghost Dance had died.

Above *To escape from the despair of agency life, the Indians turned to religion. They began to perform the Ghost Dance, often wearing symbolic "ghost shirts" like the one* **below.**

Above *A tepee stands on the island of Alcatraz against a horizon crowded by the skyscrapers of modern San Francisco.*

The white man's road

After Wounded Knee, the Indians were forced to follow the "white man's road." They remained divided into "progressives" — who tried to adopt a new life — and "traditionalists," who tried to preserve their old ways, despite schools that punished children for speaking their Indian language.

In the early 1900s the government attempted to reduce poverty among Indians by moving them into cities to find jobs, and creating industries on the reservations. However, the question of whether to make the Indians a part of white society, or allow them to live separate lives, remained. The Indians continued to face corrupt white people and racial prejudice.

The 1934 Reorganization Act allowed the Indians tribal government again, and religious freedom to perform ceremonies like the Sun Dance. In the 1950s college-educated Indians took a new pride in such traditions, and fought for compensation for lost lands.

Some young Indians, though, dismissing their elders as "apples" — red on the outside, white underneath — staged violent protests. They occupied the island of Alcatraz off San Francisco in 1969, offering the whites what they had paid for it in 1626: $24 in glass beads. Wounded Knee was also besieged for seventy-one days.

The Indian problem of adapting to a strange society remains today. It is reflected by the high rate of alcoholism, poverty and unemployment among the Indian population. The great days of Sitting Bull's people, when they dragged smoke-tanned tepees across the Mother Earth after buffalo, have gone forever. However, the Indians, who faced extinction in 1900, are now approaching their estimated original population of about one million. Their spirit has ensured survival as a people, and many have rediscovered pride of their ancestors.

Above *Today, North American Indians continue to voice a protest about their position in society.*

Left *Some, though, have adapted their culture for the benefit of tourists.*

Table of dates

1492 Christopher Columbus discovers the New World.

1539 Spanish exploration begins in the south.

1607 First permanent British colony established at Jamestown, Virginia.

1608 French settlement established in Quebec.

1620 Pilgrim Fathers land at Plymouth, Massachusetts.

1622 Indians massacre settlers in Virginia.

1670 Hudson Bay Trading Company formed.

1675 Chief Metacom leads Indians against settlers.

1680 Pueblo Revolt frees the Pueblos from Spanish rule for twelve years.

1686 William Penn's "Walking Purchase."

1763 Pontiac leads tribes against the white settlers.

1783 American settlers gain independence from Britain.

1804 Lewis & Clark expedition.

1812 Tecumseh supports British against Americans, but dies in 1813.

1830 Indian Removal Act.

1831 Sitting Bull is born.

1841 First great wagon trains on Oregon Trail.

1849 Laramie trading post becomes a fort. California gold rush.

1851 Laramie (Horse Creek) treaty.

1854 Sioux kill Grattan's soldiers.

1862 Minnesota Massacre.

1864 Sand Creek Massacre of Black Kettle's people.

1866-68 Red Cloud's War.

1867 Sitting Bull becomes chief.

1868 Black Kettle killed at Washita. Second treaty of Laramie.

1876 Battles of the Rosebud and the Little Bighorn. Indians forced to sell the Black Hills.

1877 Sitting Bull goes to Canada. Crazy Horse surrenders and is killed. The march of Chief Joseph and the Nez Percés.

1881 Sitting Bull surrenders.

1886 Geronimo surrenders.

1887 The Dawes Act divides Indian reservations.

1889-90 The Ghost Dance.

1890 Sitting Bull's death. The massacre at Wounded Knee.

1934 Indian Reorganization Act.

1969 Alcatraz occupied by militant Indians.

1973 Wounded Knee besieged.

Glossary

Agent An official from the Indian Bureau, whose job it was to manage an Indian reservation.

Breech-clout A single strip of cloth or hide worn at the waist, passed between the legs and hung front and back over a belt.

Coup (pronounced "coo") An Indian war honor. Refers particularly to touching an enemy with hand, weapon or special "coupstick."

Earth lodge An earth-covered hut used on the prairies.

Fleshing Removing flesh and tissue from hides.

Ghost Dance A religion and dance practiced from 1889-90.

Hostiles The term used by whites to describe off-reservation, independent, or raiding Indians.

Hundred-day volunteers Colorado citizens serving with the army for 100 days, often because of hatred for the Indians and a promise that they could take the possessions of the dead.

Indian police The Indians recruited to maintain order on the reservations; also called "Metal Breasts."

Jerky Dried strips of meat.

Long house A large bark-covered building used by woodland Indians.

Medicine Spiritual power bestowed upon the Indian by his gods, the Great Spirit and the Sacred Powers.

Medicine bundle A talisman or set of talismans representing and preserving the Indian's medicine.

Missionary Someone who seeks to spread his or her religious beliefs among a foreign people.

Mustangs Wild horses of North America, the descendants of strays from Spanish herds.

Nomadic Roaming from place to place.

Parfleche A waterproof rawhide wallet used mainly for holding dried food.

Pemmican Dried meat pounded with fat and berries to preserve it.

Rawhide Hide which has not been softened by tanning.

Rendezvous An annual meeting where mountain men traded furs.

Reservation An area of land reserved for the exclusive use of the Indians.

Scalp A circle of skin cut, with the attached hair, from the crown of the head. Scalping symbolized the capture of an enemy's soul. It was, in fact, a practice introduced by white settlers.

Scout A guide sent in advance of a war-party or army. The whites often employed Indians as scouts.

Sun Dance An important religious ceremony, performed by the plains tribes during the summer.

Tanning The treatment of rawhide, to soften it into leather.

Tepee (also spelled teepee, or tipi) A conical lodge of poles covered with buffalo hides, used mainly on the plains.

Totem pole A pole of tribal and individual emblems, carved by northwest coast Indians.

Travois A wooden frame based on two poles, dragged behind dogs and horses to transport belongings.

Wampum Shell beads, strung into patterns, used for rituals and money by the woodland tribes.

War bonnet A headdress with a crown and one or two streamers of eagle feathers. War bonnets of eagle feathers were also worn without streamers.

Wigwam A woodland tent or hut of hides, matting or bark.

Further information

Books

Anderson, LaVere. *Sitting Bull: Great Sioux Chief.* Easton, MD: Garrard, 1970.

Brown, Dee. *Wounded Knee: An Indian History of the American West.* New York: Holt, Rinehart & Winston, 1974.

Engel, Lorenz. *Among the Plains Indians.* Minneapolis, MN: Lerner Publications, 1970.

Fleischer, Jane. *Sitting Bull, Warrior of the Sioux.* Mahwah, NJ: Troll Associates, 1979.

Katz, Jane B., ed. *We Rode the Wind: Recollections of 19th-Century Tribal Life.* Minneapolis, MN: Lerner Publications, 1975.

Knoop, Faith Y. *Sitting Bull.* Minneapolis, MN: Dillon Press, 1974.

Nabakov, Peter, ed. *Native American Testimony: An Anthology of Indian and White Relations.* New York: Harper & Row, 1979.

Reusswig, William. *A Picture Report of the Custer Fight.* New York: Hastings House, 1967.

Sandoz, Mari. *These Were the Sioux.* Lincoln, NE: University of Nebraska Press, 1985.

Stein, R.C. *The Story of Little Bighorn.* Chicago: Childrens Press, 1983.

Picture Acknowledgments

Illustrations in this book are printed by courtesy of: the Mansell Collection 49; Peter Newark's Western Americana 13, 14, 17, 22, 26, 38, 40, 55. Other illustrations are from the Wayland Picture Library.

Index